THIS GOSPEL ACTIVITY BOOK BELONGS TO:

_____

tell us how we're doing:
coachekong00@gmail.com

Copyright 2021 LifeChangInc LLC

www.LifeChangInc.com

Author : Ukay J. Ekong

Illustrated by: Audeva Joseph

Adam & Eve

Noah's Ark

Israelites Slaves in Egypt

Let My People Go

Moses Parts Red Sea

God Gives 10 Commandments

David Plays His Harp

Shadrach, Meshach, and Abednego

Daniel in Lions Den

Jesus In The Manger

John Baptizes Jesus

Jesus is Tempted To Turn Stones To Bread

Jesus Talks To Samaritan Woman

Jesus Heals Women with Issue Of Blood

Jesus Walks On Water

Jesus Loves the Little children

Jesus A Heals Blind Man

Poor Woman Gives All She Has

The Last Supper

Jesus Carries The Cross

Jesus Is Crucified

Resurrection Day (Empty Tomb)

Jesus Appears In Garden To Mary

As the Father has loved me, so have I loved you. Now remain in my love. If you keep my commands, you will remain in my love, just as I have kept my Father's commands and remain in his love. I have told you this so that my joy maybe in you and that your joy may be complete.

John 15:9-11

Jesus Makes A Promise

Jesus Ascends Into Heaven

God Sends Holy Spirit

Paul Writes Letter From Prison

Christ Will Return As King

Write your name in Hieoglyphics!

Egyptian hieroglyphs were the formal writing system used in Ancient Egypt. Write your name in hieroglyphics.

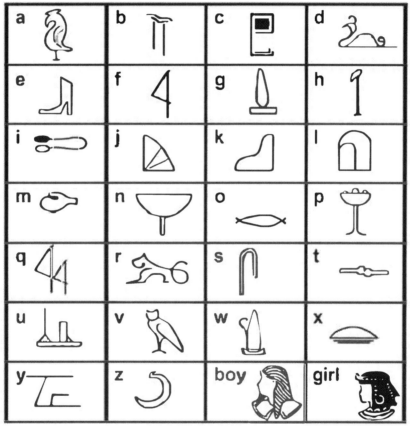

My name is

Bible crossword

Across

2 the lay members of a male religious order

3 an inspiration or divine manifestation

4 an angel portrayed as a winged child

8 of or relating to the period before the biblical flood

10 a sacrament signifying spiritual cleansing and rebirth

11 an ardent early supporter of a cause or reform

down

1 outward or visible aspect of a person or thing

2 pledged to be married

5 the act of making amends for sin or wrongdoing

6 a raised structure on which sacrifices to a god are made

7 one who believes and helps spread the doctrine of another

9 a journey by a group to escape from a hostile environment

Keyword

Bible crossword

Lorem Ipsum

Across

1 existing everywhere at once

2 any expected deliverer

5 act of attributing human characteristics to abstract ideas

7 the written body of teachings accepted by a religious group

9 a substance used to produce fermentation in dough

10 the largest or most massive thing of its kind

11 habitual eating to excess

down

1 having unlimited power

3 a delay in enforcing rights or claims or privileges

4 make furious

6 wanting in moral strength, courage, or will

8 the worship of objects or images as gods

Keyword

Who are they?

Match the bible story with the bible character

1 _____ He spent three days and nights inside a big fish.

2 _____ She married a man named Isaac.

3 _____ He was tricked by Delilah.

4 _____ He was thrown to the lions.

5 _____ He was Esau's twin brother.

6 _____ He was sold into slavery in Egypt.

7 _____ She married The king of Persia.

8 _____ He led the Israelites out of Egypt.

9 _____ He build temple in Jerusalem.

10 _____ He build a enormous boat.

A. Jacob

B. Noah

C. Esther

D. Moses

E. Salomon

F. Daniel

G. Samson

H. Joseph

I. Rebekah

J. Daniel

Bible crossword

Across

1 someone who speaks by divine inspiration

4 a state of being carried away by overwhelming emotion

5 recklessly wasteful

9 the male head of family or tribe

10 accept an excuse for

11 a prediction uttered under divine inspiration

down

2 a short moral story

3 feel happyness

6 the act of purchasing back something previously sold

6 pass from physical life

8 the worship of objects or images as gods

Keyword

Bible word search

Find the hidden words

```
t r i b u l a t i o n e w
i z h u a t w a y m n u r
p r q o v e b t e d a n a
w i l d e r n e s s t i t
n y i j h t i o u s b m h
o t u t j c s z i w a n f
e o p f o s e r m o n t y
n t l g r n e s i s r h g
c s c a p e g o a t c j o
e a t e m p e r a n c e d
a f e s t e s t i m o n y
```

scapegoat
sermon
temperance
testimony

tribulation
wilderness
wrath

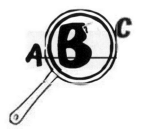

Decode the verse

Use this code to find out what God created on the 5th day of creation.

1	2	3	4	5	6	7	8	9	10	11	12	13	14	15	16	17	18	19	20	21	22	23	24	25	26
a	b	c	d	e	f	g	h	i	j	k	l	m	n	o	p	q	r	s	t	u	v	w	x	y	z

__ __ __ __ __ __ __   __ __ __ __   "__ __ __ __ __
20 8 5 14 7 15 4   19 1 9 4   12 5 20 20 8 5

__ __ __ __ __ __   __ __ __ __   __ __ __ __ __ __ __
23 1 20 5 18 19   20 5 5 13   23 9 20 8   19 23 1 18 13 19

__ __   __ __ __ __ __ __ __   __ __ __ __ __ __ __ __ __ __', __ __ __ __
15 6   12 9 22 9 14 7   3 18 5 1 20 21 18 5 19 ' 1 14 4

__ __ __   __ __ __ __ __   __ __ __   __ __ __ __ __   __ __ __
12 5 20   2 9 18 4 19   6 12 25   1 2 15 22 5   20 8 5

__ __ __ __ __   __ __   __ __ __   __ __ __ __ __   __ __ __ __ __ __ __
5 1 19 20 8   9 14   20 8 5   15 16 5 14   5 24 17 1 14 19 5

__ __   __ __ __   __ __ __ __ __ __."
15 6   20 8 5   8 5 1 22 5 14 19

__ __ __ __ __ __ __ 1:20
7 5 14 5 19 9 19

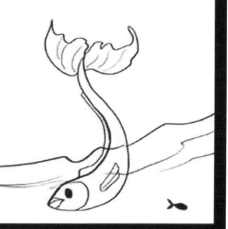

Complete the verse

Add from the box to complete each Bible verse.

All verses are fom the New International Version

1) "Heaven and _____ will pass away, but my _____ will never passs away" *(Mark 13:31)*

2) "Trust in the lord with all your _____ and lean not on your own _____ ; in all your _____ Submit to him, and he will make your path _____" *(Proberbs 3:5-6)*

3) "...God has said, " Never will i _____ you; never will i _____ you" *(hebrews 13:5)*

4) "For we are God's Handiwork, created in _____ Jesus To do _____ Works, wich God pepared in advance for us to do" *(Ephesian 2 : 10)*

5) "Ask and it will be _____ to you; seek and you will _____ Knock and the door will be _____ to you" *(Matthew 7:7)*

heart
Forsake
Christ
given
good
earth
opened
straight
leave
find
ways
words
understanding

Who is Mary?

Read the scriptures below
Put the letter on the right next to the correct answer on the left

1 _____ The angel Gabriel announces to Mary she will have a special son

2 _____ She married a man named Joseph.

3 _____ She is Jesus's mother.

4 _____ She presents Jesus at the Temple on the 8th day.

5 _____ She escapes to Egypt with Joseph and Jesus.

6 _____ She scolds Jesus for staying at the temple after the feast of Unleavened Bread.

7 _____ She attends a wedding in Cana with Jesus.

8 _____ She waits at Golgotha when Jesus was crucified.

9 _____ She joins the diciples in Jerusalem after Jesus's death.

A. Luke 2:7

B. Luke 2: 41-50

C. Matthew 2:14

D. John 2: 1-12

E. Luke 1: 30-33

F. John 19: 25

G. Acts 1:13

H. Luke 2: 22

I. Matthew 1: 24

Through the maze

trace the path through the armor of God

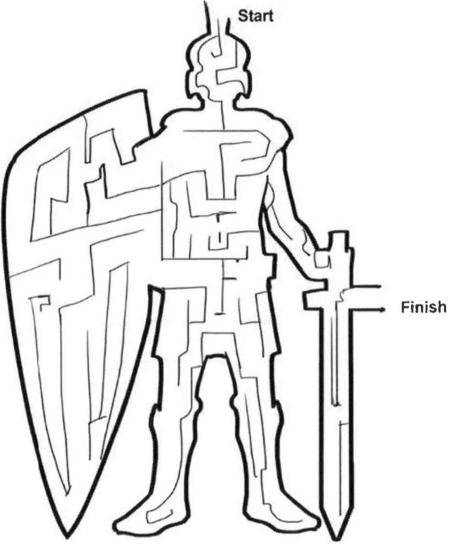

" Stand firm then, with the belt of truth buckled around your waist, with the breastplate of righteousness in place.and with your feet fitted with the readiness that comes from the gospel of peace. In addition to all this, take up the shield of faith, with which you can extinguish all the flaming arrows of the evil one. Take the helmet of salvation and the sword of the Spirit, which is the word of God."

Ephesians 6:14-17

Will it Grow?

Add the number in the box to get the code number for each letter. Then solve the puzzle

a	17+34 = ____
b	28+44 = ____
c	39+57 = ____
d	16+65 = ____
e	62+37 = ____
f	41+38 = ____
g	24+33 = ____
h	47+29 = ____
i	24+58 = ____
l	41+25 = ____
n	23+15 = ____
o	29+49 = ____
p	22+11 = ____
r	55+34 = ____
s	29+16 = ____
t	44+26 = ____
u	13+14 = ____
v	23+68 = ____
w	23+19 = ____
y	36+25 = ____

__ __ __   __ __ __   __ __ __ __   __ __
72 27 70   70 76 99   45 99 99 81   78 38

__ __ __ __   __ __ __ __   __ __ __ __ __ __
57 78 78 81   45 78 82 66   45 70 51 38 81 45

__ __ __   __ __ __ __ __   __ __ __ __   __
79 78 89   70 76 78 45 99   42 82 70 76   51

__ __ __ __ __   __ __ __   __ __ __ __
38 78 72 66 99   51 38 81   57 78 78 81

__ __ __ __ __   __ __ __   __ __ __ __   __ __ __
76 99 51 89 70   42 76 78   76 99 51 89   70 76 99

__ __ __ __ __'   __ __ __ __ __ __   __ __'   __ __ __
42 78 89 81   89 99 70 51 82 38   82 70   51 38 81

__ __   __ __ __ __ __ __ __ __ __ __ __ __
72 61   33 99 89 45 99 91 99 89 82 38 57

(Luke 8:15)

__ __ __ __ __ __ __   __   __ __ __ __
33 89 78 81 27 96 94   51   96 89 78 33

Through the maze

Help the good sherpherd leave the 90 and 9 sheep safely in the fold and go find this one lost sheep

"I am the good shepherd. The good shepherd lays down his life for the sheep."
John 10:11

Bible word search

Find the hidden words

```
r b a s a c r i f i c e r
e z r u g t x a y o n u e
p r a d v e n t e t a n v
e j i s o l u s i a t e e
n r i g h t e o u s t v l
t t u t n c s z i w a n a
e o p f i b o n n e t o t
n l g e n e s i s r h i
c y a e p r o h p b c a o
e a h r s e i d i s i p n
b r e s u r e c t i o n r
```

Genesis
advent
repentance
resurrection

revelation
righteous
sacrifice

who are they?

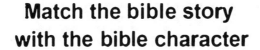

Match the bible story with the bible character

1. __J__ He spent three days and nights inside a big fish.

2. __I__ She married a man named Isaac.

3. __E__ He was tricked by Delilah.

4. __F__ He was thrown to the lions.

5. __A__ He was Esau's twin brother.

6. __H__ He was sold into slavery in Egypt.

7. __C__ She married The king of Persia.

8. __D__ He led the Israelites out of Egypt.

9. __G__ He build temple in Jerusalem.

10. __D__ He build a enormous boat.

A. Jacob
B. Noah
C. Esther
D. Moses
E. Salomon
F. Daniel
G. Samson
H. Joseph
I. Rebekah
J. Jonah

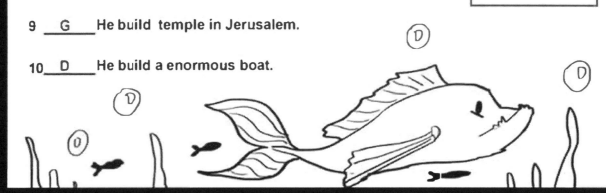

altar : a raised structure on which sacrifices to a god are made
antediluvian : of or relating to the period before the biblical flood
apostle : an ardent early supporter of a cause or reform
appearance : outward or visible aspect of a person or thing
atonement : the act of making amends for sin or wrongdoing
baptism : a sacrament signifying spiritual cleansing and rebirth
betrothed : pledged to be married
brethren : the lay members of a male religious order
cherub : an angel portrayed as a winged child
disciple : one who believes and helps spread the doctrine of another
epiphany : an inspiration or divine manifestation
exodus : a journey by a group to escape from a hostile environment
fallible : wanting in moral strength, courage, or will
forbearance :a delay in enforcing rights or claims or privileges
gluttony : habitual eating to excess
gospel : the written body of teachings accepted by a religious group
idolatry : the worship of objects or images as gods
incarnation: act of attributing human characteristics to abstract ideas
incense :make furious
leaven : a substance used to produce fermentation in dough
leviathan : the largest or most massive thing of its kind
messiah: any expected deliverer
omnipotent : having unlimited power
omnipresent :existing everywhere at once
parable : a short moral story
paradise : any place of complete bliss and delight and peace
pardon : accept an excuse for
patriarch: the male head of family or tribe
perish: pass from physical life
pestilence: any epidemic disease with a high death rate
prodigal: recklessly wasteful
prophecy : a prediction uttered under divine inspiration
prophet: someone who speaks by divine inspiration
rapture: a state of being carried away by overwhelming emotion
redemption: the act of purchasing back something previously sold
rejoice : feel happiness

Bible crossword

Across

2 the lay members of a male religious order

3 an inspiration or divine manifestation

4 an angel portrayed as a winged child

8 of or relating to the period before the biblical flood

10 a sacrament signifying spiritual cleansing and rebirth

11 an ardent early supporter of a cause or reform

down

1 outward or visible aspect of a person or thing

2 pledged to be married

5 the act of making amends for sin or wrongdoing

6 a raised structure on which sacrifices to a god are made

7 one who believes and helps spread the doctrine of another

9 a journey by a group to escape from a hostile environment

Keyword

Crossword grid solution

Across:
- 2: BETHREN
- 3: EPIPHANY
- 4: CHERUB
- 8: ANTEDILUVIAN
- 10: BAPTISM
- 11: APOSTLE

Down:
- 1: APPEARANCE
- 2: BETHROTHED
- 5: ATONEMENT
- 6: ALTAR
- 7: DICIPLE
- 9: EXODUS

Bible crossword

Lorem Ipsum

Across

1 existing everywhere at once

2 any expected deliverer

5 act of attributing human characteristics to abstract ideas

7 the written body of teachings accepted by a religious group

9 a substance used to produce fermentation in dough

10 the largest or most massive thing of its kind

11 habitual eating to excess

down

1 having unlimited power

3 a delay in enforcing rights or claims or privileges

4 make furious

6 wanting in moral strength, courage, or will

8 the worship of objects or images as gods

Keyword

Bible word search

Find the hidden words

t	r	i	b	u	l	a	t	i	o	n	e	w
i	z	h	u	a	t	w	a	y	m	n	u	r
p	r	q	o	v	e	b	t	e	d	a	n	a
w	i	l	d	e	r	n	e	s	s	t	i	t
n	y	i	j	h	t	i	o	u	s	b	m	h
o	t	u	t	j	c	s	z	i	w	a	n	f
e	o	p	f	o	s	e	r	m	o	n	t	y
n	t	l	g	r	n	e	s	i	s	r	h	g
c	s	c	a	p	e	g	o	a	t	c	j	o
e	a	t	e	m	p	e	r	a	n	c	e	d
a	f	e	s	t	e	s	t	i	m	o	n	y

scapegoat ✓
sermon ✓
temperance
testimony ✓

tribulation ✓
wilderness ✓
wrath ✓

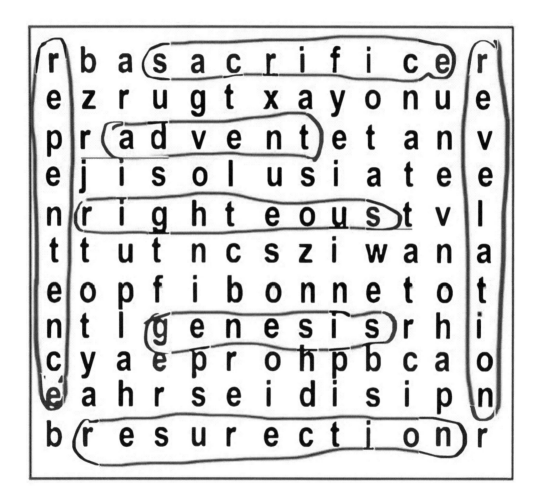

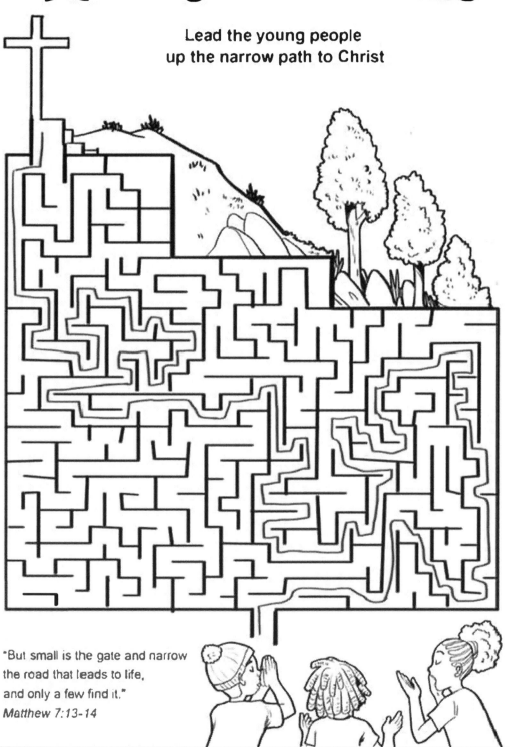

Through the maze

trace the path through the armor of God

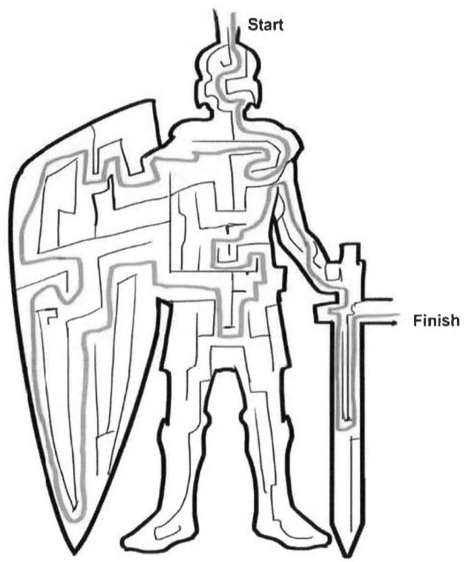

" Stand firm then, with the belt of truth buckled around your waist, with the breastplate of righteousness in place,and with your feet fitted with the readiness that comes from the gospel of peace. In addition to all this, take up the shield of faith, with which you can extinguish all the flaming arrows of the evil one. Take the helmet of salvation and the sword of the Spirit, which is the word of God."

Ephesians 6:14-17

Complete the verse

Add from the box to complete each Bible verse.
All verses are fom the New International Version

1) "Heaven and ___earth___ will pass away, but my ___words___ will never passs away" *(Mark 13:31)*

2) "Trust in the lord with all your ___heart___ and lean not on your own ___understanding___; in all your ___ways___ Submit to him, and he will make your path ___straight___" *(Proberbs 3:5-6)*

3) "...God has said, " Never will I ___leave___ you; never will i ___Forsake___ you" *(hebrews 13:5)*

4) "For we are God's Handiwork, created in ___Christ___ Jesus To do ___good___ Works, wich God pepared in advance for us to do" *(Ephesian 2 : 10)*

5) "Ask and it will be ___given___ to you; seek and you will ___find___ Knock and the door will be ___opened___ to you" *(Matthew 7:7)*

heart
Forsake
Christ
given
good
earth
opened
straight
leave
find
ways
words
understanding

Decode the verse

Use this code to find out what God created on the 5th day of creation.

1	2	3	4	5	6	7	8	9	10	11	12	13	14	15	16	17	18	19	20	21	22	23	24	25	26
a	b	c	d	e	f	g	h	i	j	k	l	m	n	o	p	q	r	s	t	u	v	w	x	y	z

then God said "let the

waters teem with swarms

of living creatures, and

let birds fly above the

earth in the open expanse

of the heavens."

genesis 1:20

Bible crossword

Across

1 someone who speaks by divine inspiration

4 a state of being carried away by overwhelming emotion

5 recklessly wasteful

7 any epidemic disease with high death rate

9 the male head of family or tribe

10 accept an excuse for

11 a prediction uttered under divine inspiration

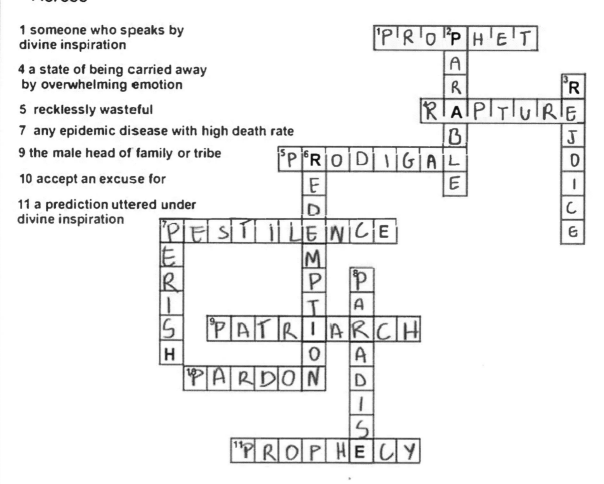

down

2 a short moral story

3 feel happyness

6 the act of purchasing back something previously sold

7 pass from physical life

8 any place of complete bliss and delight and peace

Keyword

Who are they?

Match the bible story with the bible character

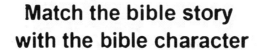

1. __J__ He spent three days and nights inside a big fish.

2. __I__ She married a man named Isaac.

3. __E__ He was tricked by Delilah.

4. __F__ He was thrown to the lions.

5. __A__ He was Esau's twin brother.

6. __H__ He was sold into slavery in Egypt.

7. __C__ She married The king of Persia.

8. __D__ He led the Israelites out of Egypt.

9. __G__ He build temple in Jerusalem.

10. __D__ He build a enormous boat.

A. Jacob
B. Noah
C. Esther
D. Moses
E. Salomon
F. Daniel
G. Samson
H. Joseph
I. Rebekah
J. Jonah

Through the maze

Help the good sherpherd leave the 90 and 9 sheep safely in the fold and go find this one lost sheep

"I am the good shepherd. The good shepherd lays down his life for the sheep."
John 10:11

Who is Mary?

Read the scriptures below
Put the letter on the right next
to the correct answer on the left

1. __E__ The angel Gabriel announces to Mary she will have a special son

2. __I__ She married a man named Joseph.

3. __A__ She is Jesus's mother.

4. __H__ She presents Jesus at the Temple on the 8th day.

5. __C__ She escapes to Egypt with Joseph and Jesus.

6. __B__ She scolds Jesus for staying at the temple after the feast of Unleavened Bread.

7. __D__ She attends a wedding in Cana with Jesus.

8. __F__ She waits at Golgotha when Jesus was crucified.

9. __G__ She joins the diciples in Jerusalem after Jesus's death.

A. Luke 2:7
B. Luke 2: 41-50
C. Matthew 2:14
D. John 2: 1-12
E. Luke 1: 30-33
F. John 19: 25
G. Acts 1:13
H. Luke 2: 22
I. Matthew 1: 24

Will it Grow?

Add the number in the box to get the code number for each letter.
Then solve the puzzle

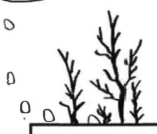

a	17+34 =	51
b	28+44 =	72
c	39+57 =	94
d	16+65 =	81
e	62+37 =	99
f	41+38 =	79
g	24+33 =	57
h	47+29 =	76
i	24+58 =	82
l	41+25 =	66
n	23+15 =	38
o	29+49 =	78
p	22+11 =	33
r	55+34 =	89
s	29+16 =	45
t	44+26 =	70
u	13+14 =	27
v	23+68 =	91
w	23+19 =	42
y	36+25=	61

b u t   t h e   s e e d   o n
72 27 70 70 76 99 45 99 99 81 78 38

g o o d   s o i l   s t a n d s
57 78 78 81 45 78 82 66 45 70 51 38 81 45

f o r   t h o s e   w i t h   a
79 78 89 70 76 78 45 99 42 82 70 76 51

n o b l e   a n d   g o o d
38 78 72 66 99 51 38 81 57 78 78 81

h e a r t   w h o   h e a r   t h e
76 99 51 89 70 42 76 78 76 99 51 89 70 76 99

w o r d,   r e t a i n   i t,   a n d
42 78 89 81 89 99 70 51 82 38 82 70 51 38 81

b y   p e r s e v e r i n g
72 61 33 99 89 45 99 91 99 89 82 38 57

p r o d u c a   a   c r o p.   (Luke 8:15)
33 89 78 81 27 96 94 51 96 89 78 33

God Bless You!

Isaiah 41:10

Made in the USA
Middletown, DE
29 January 2024

48585148R00051